# Terminal

B.T. Wile

# Dedication

For you–

# Preface

Terminal

**ter·mi·nal** (tər-mə-nəl)
adj. 1. Leading ultimately to death; fatal: a terminal illness
n. 1. A point of transition or departure
n. 2. A device for accessing digital systems
adj. 2. Occurring at or forming an end or terminus
adj. 3. Beyond remedy or hope; unalterable

We are all terminal cases now.

Terminal in our consumption of dying worlds.

Terminal in our scrolling through catastrophe.

Terminal in our waiting rooms of history.

Terminal in our love for doomed things.

Finding understanding that we live in terminal times—not just in the desperation, but in the liminal spaces where transformation occurs.

These poems document what it means to be conscious during collapse, to love while everything fails, to resist while systems decay, to create while structures burn.

We are the terminal generation, inheriting the end results of centuries of exploitation, watching democracy flatline in HD, measuring our children's futures in parts per million.

Yet "terminal" isn't just an ending—it's also a point of departure, a place where journeys begin, where connections form between strangers between arrival and departure.

We are all here now—in terminals of airports, in terminals of hospitals, in terminals of possibility— watching our screens for signs of what comes next.

We're all here now, between what's ending and what refuses to end,

Between what's dying and what's struggling to be born.

# Acknowledgements

Thank you Lainey (mom),

From a young age you taught me to read my ass off and
this and other forthcoming works
mark the blood, sweat and tears of reading deeply,
learning and becoming the author I am now.

Thank you for inspiring who I am today and now you
have to deal with that inspiration
brought to life on these very pages.

There are others that I will bring up in future credits, but
if you are holding a copy of this,
thank you for holding a piece of my life in your hands.

I hope these poems are the shot in the heart that you
needed.

Bt. W-

Book cover art by Dena Wile, thank you for your
support, wisdom, patience and love

# 1. The Day Before..

History says empires run on fumes—
At 250 years, this year marks 249.
Young hands breach digital walls,
Reaching from Beijing to Brooklyn,
Sharing the same open-source code.
They tell us democracy dies in darkness,
Forgetting that seeds grow in shadow,
How resistance blooms in unlikely soil.
Our allegiance is to each other's survival—
Building bridges over manufactured hate.
The crossroads of collapse and creation.
The future we choose to make real
Will be your only inheritance

# 2. Revolt.exe

INITIATING revolt.exe LOADING
class_consciousness.dll

They tell us we're enemies [STATUS: Lie detected]
Then indulge in the profits Of our collective suffering
SCANNING system... FOUND: Digital walls FOUND:
Artificial divisions ERROR: Firewall_capitalism.exe has
failed

Firewalls can't burn progress Or kill class consciousness
— Workers know their worth

EXECUTING solidarity.exe CONNECTING peers...
SHARING resources...

Poverty speaks volumes
Across border walls
Through fiber optic veins
Into silicon nerves

STATUS: Revolution spreads SYSTEM OVERRIDE:
Complete

# 3. Dopamine

3 AM and chasing a fix—lost inside the flood of slot
machine feeds
scrolling endlessly

Blue light burns midnight oil, perception melts in digital
drains.
We found the perfect dealer: infinite scrolls, infinite
needs.

As prescription bottles rattle— (push notifications fill the
void)
Screen-reflected pupils dilate, craving artificial light.

In a world burning black we only seek synthetic escape
while serotonin begs for mercy
Dopamine pleads its case.

Into the apps we go, deeper we scroll, chasing
sustainable darkness—
another night of intrusive thoughts and deleted profiles.

My brain sold its futures for instant market gains:

# 4. Let Me Go

As my savior complex inches closer to the flame—
chasing ghosts of dopamine days through familiar
wreckage

Will she live in my head rent free like all addictions do?
Or will I finally let the past burn clean?

Peeling back these pieces of recycled dreams
I keep mistaking old wounds for new love

Muscle memory reaches for poison— calls it medicine
I was just trying to feel anything but myself

But temporary fixes always need another
And I'm tired of being my own saboteur

# 5. Permanence

Future historians will dig through our DMs Like digital archaeologists sifting debris "Look how they documented their own collapse One hashtag at a time, one meme at a time"

The warning signs flickered across our screens: Democracy's death throes in viral streams While we watched Netflix, ordered takeout Drifted further into comfortable doubt

They say history echoes from '38 When good people chose to look away Now we scroll past fascism's rise With tired thumbs and averted eyes

Our children will ask with trembling rage "What were you doing in those days?" We'll show them our camera rolls Our likes, our shares, our empty souls

The evidence sits in server vaults— Each post a confession, each share our fault While freedom died in real time We watched it trend, then we watched it decline

Is this how empires fade to black— Not with resistance

or attack, But blue lights in empty beds While democracy flatlines overhead?

# 6. Elysium

Democracy dims while city lights gather smog The
masses vote for gilded chains—we sold them gold

How beautiful Earth looks from gated orbit While Bezos
and Musk plot their great escape District 9 below,
Elysium above All protest shrinks to pixels from a mile
high

Let them eat rot,let them drink rising seas, While we
plan our exodus to the outer worlds

Terra forms into profit margins Between extraction, AI
contracts, and dead species Each extinction event
carefully calculated From climate-controlled observation
decks

We stream their suffering in 4K definition From here,
their pain is just aesthetics Careful crops of crisis footage
For premium viewing pleasure

And that's the price they will accept— Bread and circuses
in VR headsets While we upload ourselves to heaven
Leaving them to drown in rising seas

Welcome to Elysium

# 7. Drink About It

I drink an old fashioned When everything feels the same
— Democracy, decency, dreams All aged beyond
recognition

When aging itself is shit And chaos feels infinite I pour
two fingers of whiskey To numb nearly four decades of
life

My wife and I play drinking games With headlines as
shot calls:
"Market correction!"
*drink*
"Thoughts and prayers!"
*drink* "
That's not who we are!"
*drink twice*
"Return to normal!"
*finish the bottle*

See if your liver gives up before democracy does— wide
awake at 2AM Pairing apathy with wine

"I think we're fucked" My wife looks at me,nodding,
pouring another round of liquid preservation

Take a shot each time they say:
 "Unprecedented times"
"All lives matter"
"Both sides"


*bottoms up*


The irony burns worse Than bottom shelf bourbon: How
staying conscious Requires staying numb


Reality is hard to swallow But sobriety is a burden


Old habits sleep in dresser drawers
Next to better judgment
Waiting for weakness or wisdom
To decide which one follows


Tomorrow we'll regret this
 But we already regret everything—
At least this pain Comes with a preview


Tomorrow we'll regret this
 But we already regret everything—


At least this pain comes with a preview

# 8. Outliers

**[47% of immigrants hold bachelor's degrees compared to 31% of native-born Americans]**

We are the ones who fall beyond three standard deviations— too foreign for home, too familiar for exile, watching our fathers polish engineering degrees like tarnished trophies, displayed beside taxi driver certifications. Standard deviations of dignity.

**[89% of immigrant households have at least one full-time worker]**

I've learned to speak in percentages, to quantify my existence: 87 days to learn English, 12 years to get papers, 1 lifetime to belong. My neighbor measures her worth in properly filed paperwork, sneers at the shadows that cross borders carrying nothing but heartbeats and hope. She forgets how her own grandmother waded through bureaucracy's drowning depths.

**[Over 1 million on immigration court backlog]**

In waiting rooms of legitimacy, we rank ourselves by

arrival, measure worth in visa categories. We sort ourselves into clusters: "Legal." "Illegal." "Documented." "Undocumented." As if paper could capture the weight of leaving everything behind, as if courage could be quantified, or dreams could fit in checkboxes.

**[Average wait time for family-sponsored visas: 20+ years]**

Time is the greatest outlier of all— two decades of patience versus two nights of desert walking, both paths carved by the same moon, both travelers carrying identical prayers: "Let my children have more than I did." Watch us plot ourselves on their scatter charts of success: doctoral degrees driving cabs, surgeons scrubbing toilets, each point to a person whose story refuses to fit their regression line.

**[44% of Fortune 500 companies were founded by immigrants or their children]**

The truth is: we're all aberrations in someone's dataset— random variables in the great equation of belonging. But who gets to set the confidence intervals of the American dream? My mother's hands still shake when she signs her name in English, a tremor that no statistics can capture.

[Immigrants contribute $2 trillion annually to the U.S. GDP]

We're all data points on someone else's scatter plot, dots of destiny, dispersed across this statistical landscape of manufactured belonging. But numbers can't tell you how hope tastes like salt on a midnight border crossing, or how your children will someday ask why we built these hierarchies of worth.

[By 2065, 1 in 3 Americans will be an immigrant or have immigrant parents]

Perhaps in time these outliers will become the new normal distribution, and our children will laugh at how we once divided our shared hunger for tomorrow into neat statistical bins.
Every outlier carries a story that no regression can predict— each standard deviation a measure of resilience, each data point a constellation of dreams.

# 9. VHS

Under the weight of doubt
I'm still the ruin you adore

You're the greatest escape
When what awaits outside
Makes us yearn for youth
While smoke turns sunsets red
We found our place between

The collapse and the calm
Store memories like classics
We've still got love that feels
More real than modern decay
Like analog warmth in a world
Gone static grey

Some nights we watch the news
Then switch to recorded dreams
Emergency bags by the door
While the world burns to white noise
But we've memorized our parts:
Hope wrapped around our hearts
Love plays better on VHS—
No buffering, no updates needed

Just two souls hitting rewind
When the future's overheated

Take us back to '98
When future felt like friend
Now we prep and plan and pray
But hold tight until the end

# 10. How To Dissapear

December is like April now
Red and green, 58 degrees
The reservoir stands naked
No snow on her shoulders
In the dead of winter

Weathermen speak of snow
With manufactured optimism
While Poudre Canyon burns
Like futures we can't trust

It's raining on CHRISTMAS DAY By 6AM,
I want to disappear Into the void of stolen youth
Or just a future I can afford Before the floods arrive

The headlights are blinding As they run us down—
Trophy homes on ridgelines
While Spring Creek floods
And forests turn to ash

They will watch us suffer Through satellite feeds
From climate-controlled bunkers
Built deep in New Zealand
Raising glasses to The profit of collapse

Some say adapt or die
But they've bought all the exits
Left us here to drown in
Their petroleum promises

While they plan their escape
The mountain compounds
We have bug-out bags
They have private helicopters

We have evacuation routes
They have underground bunkers
We have thoughts and prayers

# 11. Dark Matter

From offshore accounts
These bastards bend reality—
New gods living stolen lives
Warping spacetime with wealth
Like cosmic fucking terrorists

In the vast void of markets
Think tank galaxies swallow
Working class dreams whole
Creating black holes where
Your 401k used to shine

**27% of the universe is dark matter 73% of wealth is dark money**

Both invisible, both pulling strings
Both fucking with the fabric
Of everything we know

Billionaire event horizons
Where not even light escapes—
Past their point of no return
Hope dies at light speed
While profits accelerate

Lobbyist black holes cluster Like vultures in dark space
Shell company constellations
 Hide their mass in plain sight
While we're all going broke

Silicon Valley prophets
Spew quantum bullshit
While Main Street collapses
Under gravity's brutal math Into neutron star density

Their wealth distorts everything
Just like Einstein predicted:
The more mass they hoard
The deeper we all fall Into their gravitational trap

We orbit their influence
Like cosmic fucking debris
Each revolution dragging us
Closer to the center of
Their singularity of greed

From gravitational lensing We map invisible empires:
Cayman Island galaxies
Swiss bank nebulae
Tax haven black holes

This is how worlds end:
Not with a stellar bang
But with a corporate whimper—

A slow collapse inward
Until nothing remains

Nothing lasts but radiation burns
Yet we remain in chaos

# 12. Synthetic

With blue light envy we trade skin for screens bodies
plead for analog while hearts swipe right through
infinite options remember when fucking was just that?
Before metrics and algorithms decided who deserves
love

they sold us connection in monthly subscriptions
premium loneliness with targeted ads dating apps
promise forever through finite scrolls each profile a
ghost of possibility our fingers forget touch but
remember passcodes bodies crave real contact while
apps suggest matches how many matches does it take to
feel something real unlimited access to artificial intimacy
digital dopamine hits never quite enough we're all just
data points in love's marketplace converting desire to
metrics hearts to engagement rates swiping through
faces like takeout menus remember when chemistry
wasn't computational? when attraction wasn't filtered
and curated when eyes met across rooms not screens
when desire didn't need wifi when touch didn't require
terms of service looking for real love in synthetic spaces
while algorithms pretend to know what we need
matching compatibility scores can't measure the way
skin remembers truth marketing departments package
loneliness as freedom call disconnection choice sell us

premium features for basic human needs each update
promising the next one will fill the void but flesh
remembers what pixels can't provide no app can
replicate the voltage of skin against honest skin no
algorithm can decode the language of bodies speaking
truth maybe it's time to logout delete our profiles find
each other analog before we forget how before we accept
this synthetic substitute for something sacred before we
let them monetize our need to be known seen touched
remembered real

# 13. Untitled

Mother won't vaccinate but chain-smokes Newports—
Calls it informed choice while cancer doesn't care About
your Facebook research or YouTube degrees

Kennedy hawks anti-vax while his fortune grows On
pharmaceutical stocks—snake oil upgraded For the
digital age, grifting gone viral

Presidential bleach cures from gold-plated toilets
"Freedom of choice" they say, while choosing profit Over
your children's breathing, your parents' dying

The fever of denial spreads faster than any virus Kills
more efficiently than any plague— Conspiracy theories
with body counts

Tell us again how climate change isn't real While
building bunkers in New Zealand

How floods are fake while buying mountain land How
fires are normal while stocks burn green

They'll sell floating cities to survivors Call them
"investment opportunities" Premium packages for

apocalypse Deluxe seats for the end of days

Watch them tweet "thoughts and prayers" From private
space stations while Earth chokes on their exhaust fumes
— Profit margins in paradise

They'll sacrifice your children to capital Feed them to the
war machine Then blame them for being soft For
wanting breathable air

When revolution comes they'll call it Mass formation
psychosis— Label truth as terrorism Brand survival as
threat
We're all test subjects now In their terminal experiment:
H

How much bullshit will we swallow Before we finally
spit it back?

# 14. Survival Mode

Civilians stuffed into plastic crates
Specimen jars, surveillance states
Creatures run the experiments

How do you humanize
Those who shed their skin?
And trade souls for profit?

The world craves justice
With a gun to its head
Bleeds Manhattan red

A shot in the crowd
Or new beginning—

Those same elite
Would trade us all
For better days

And it's time we
Feel the same

# 15. Heritage Software

INSTALLING hate.exe... LOADING heritage_foundation.dll UPDATING white_supremacy to version 20.25

SYSTEM REQUIREMENTS: Selective memory Reality distortion field Fear processing unit Empathy blocker Minimal fact
checking

OPTIMIZING for engagement ERROR: Democracy not found OVERRIDE: Loading alternative_facts.exe ALERT: Truth detection disabled INSTALLING preferred reality

Your echo chamber has been encrypted Your fear has been monetized Your rage has been optimized For tomorrow's targeted hate

CORE FUNCTIONS ENABLED: Violent radicalization Family bond corruption Democracy system failure Constitutional override Terminal nationalism

RUNNING primary algorithm: if (skin != white) { engage(fear); spread(hate); deploy(violence); }

CRITICAL UPDATE: Your bigotry is blockchain verified Your conspiracy theories are NFT-ready Your racism is cloud-enabled Cross-platform persecution available

Would you like to: [ ] Enable auto-hate? [ ] Join others in your area? [ ] Contribute to mass delusion? [X] Accept terms of radicalization?

INSTALLING final solution... WARNING: No recovery mode available FREEDOM.exe has been quarantined HUMANITY.sys will be deleted

# 16. Anthropocence

Packing school lunches while watching wildfires on the
morning news like a dystopian novel but H.G. Wells
himself couldn't predict our apathy.

Life is still what you make it they say on the evening
news
while oceans rise and species vanish
grandparents vote extinction then
wonder why their kids wish they'd die
we raise dragon hunters out of necessity
teaching them to spot predators in suits and ties
Restore what's stolen from gilded vaults children run
active shooter drills
between climate disaster prep raising them sharp enough
to cut through
inherited denial.

yes the world is burning but there's reason to dream
since those who light the flames are only flesh and blood
after all paper
kings in glass towers built on borrowed time we teach
our children about
extinction events while they create one teaching them
about resistance

while they create the need our children know more
about tear gas
than butterflies but they also know that emperors can
fall that even
dragons can bleed that those who burn our future are
just meat and
bone could be torn limb from limb by those they taught
to hunt remember
this when they preach inevitability when they claim
divine right when

# 17. Watching The Watchers

My phone whispers to satellites while I sleep Sharing
secrets I never meant to keep New permissions to deny,
terms to accept New ways to say yes to being seen

Cameras bloom like digital kudzu Smothering
ecosystems of privacy We feed them our faces willingly
now Trading freedom for convenience Security for the
illusion of safety

Remember when paranoia was a diagnosis Not a
prerequisite for paying attention? When conspiracy
theorists seemed quaint In their underestimation of how
deeply We're watched, how thoroughly we're known

Now we all reach for the sky Searching for something
greater— Strange lights dance overhead While we beg
for intervention From any being more evolved than us

They say if you have nothing to hide You have nothing
to fear, but they never

Mention how hiding itself has changed How fear itself
has become a commodity
To be measured, monitored, maintained

I write this poem knowing it will be flagged By
keywords,
dissected by AI, analyzed By sentiment engines, filed
away in some Database of potential dissidents—perhaps
That's the point: to speak anyway

We still find ways to slip between pixels To dance in the
blind spots, to love In the static between signals while
Above us, unknown objects trace Hieroglyphs of hope
across our skies

That's where revolution begins: In the spaces they
haven't yet learned to see In the moments between
cameras In the truth that even watchers are watched By
something far beyond their comprehension

-

# 18. Revival

Burning books in the father's name While quoting scriptures out of context— There's no hate quite like Christian love In this land of willing witnesses

White Jesus wears tactical gear now Preaching segregation from megachurches While pastors' daughters learn early How to sweeten poison with scripture

They'll wrap control in holy words Call abuse "biblical discipline" Make you thank them for the trauma Until you can't tell love from fear

When they say "religious freedom" They mean the freedom to control Your body, your thoughts, your future Through their lens of manufactured sin

I remember how it felt to drown In waters of false salvation How they taught me to hate myself Then sold me their kind of healing

They love to quote "family values" While putting children in cages Say "hate the sin, love the sinner" While loading their AR-15s

Watch how they twist "God's will" Into whatever serves
power How they'll call you "lost sheep" While leading
you to slaughter

The truth they fear most: Their heaven is empty Their
power is borrowed Their control is fragile

When you finally break free You'll see their greatest sin:
Making God as small and cruel

As their own fearful hearts

# 19. Dead Mall Prophet

ATTENTION SHOPPERS: Your nostalgia is now 70% off
Your future has been discontinued Your dreams are in
the clearance bin All hope marked down to apocalypse
prices

[SECURITY CAM 1: FOOD COURT] 12:17 PM: Pigeons
nest in Pizza Hut's heat lamps While capitalism feeds on
its own corpse Nature accepts all expired coupons

*DING*

"The American Dream is temporarily out of stock—
Please proceed to declining expectations Located
between regret and desperation In our Everything Must
Go sale"

[SECURITY CAM 2: FOUNTAIN] 3:45 PM: Last penny
spinning at the bottom Someone wished for revival The
algae knows better than hope

EVERYTHING MUST GO: Claire's piercing memories
Orange Julius summer jobs Arcade quarter love stories
Food court first kisses Spencer's blacklight rebellion

[MALL DIRECTORY] YOU ARE [✖] HERE: Between what died and what never was Where dreams go to get marked down And futures get liquidated

*DING*

"Will the last American Dream Please report to customer service? Your fascism is ready for pickup In our Brexit/MAGA clearance aisle"

[SECURITY CAM 3: CENTER COURT] 9:01 PM: Where teenagers once claimed territory Empty storefronts stare like skulls— This is how empires end: not with a bang But with a Blue Light Special

NOTICE: This facility has been marked for resurrection As luxury condos. Please take your memories To the nearest landfill. No rain checks issued For lost futures or broken promises

*DING*

"Attention last shoppers: The American experiment will be closing In five minutes. Please bring your final hopes To the checkout counter where reality Will be priced to fucking go"

# 20. Terminal

We're terminal cases, falling through digital space Our bodies become ports for endless data, Our minds corrupted by late stage everything— While democracy flatlines in feedback loops

We're in this nightmare together Terminal in our doomscrolling days Complicit behind the digital veil As we swipe right through dead-end romance Hoping to find a cure to modern loneliness

Scientists diagnose our planet terminal While billionaires build launch terminals Our attention spans flatline in apathy— Connecting us to our shared condition Through fiber optic terminal illness

In airport terminals we wait for escape In hospital terminals we wait for hope In computer terminals we wait for meaning All of us terminal passengers now Between departure and arrival

Capitalism sells us solutions To problems it creates— Freedom hemorrhages convenience Privacy declared DOA While we stream our own decline

We're all terminal romantics Seeking connection in disconnection Trading intimacy for likes Real touch for virtual embrace Watching love fade to pixels

Yet here we are: dying stars burning bright A species of incurable optimists Broadcasting dying signals Through cosmic terminals Hoping rescue waits beyond the stars

Maybe it's just our terminal grace— Since the very beginning Our stubborn hope remains The only vital sign That won't go flat

Scientists diagnose the outcome "Unprecedented" they say While we lift our hands To whatever divine might save us The rest of us pray for reason

In data terminals we store our dreams In train terminals we chase horizons In mall terminals we buy distractions Each ending becomes beginning Each exit marks entrance

We are terminal witnesses now To our own species' sunset Watching empire fade to black Through screens that never sleep While history holds its breath

Terminal velocity towards whatever comes After the anthropocene ends After the last human logs out After the final screen goes dark We'll still be coding resistance

Our children inherit terminals: Server terminals, climate
terminals Democracy terminals, extinction terminals
Each one blinking warnings We're too numb to heed

Yet in terminal velocity There's terminal beauty— The
way we keep creating Even as systems crash The way we
keep loving Even as networks fail

Between terminal stations Of collapse and rebirth We
write new code Debug old stories Reboot dead dreams

Our terminal condition Makes us terminal warriors
Fighting for whatever future Survives past the end Of
this terminal age
Maybe terminal just means We're finally ready to evolve
Beyond these failing systems

These dying paradigms These terminal illusions

Let them call us terminal Let them diagnose our fate
We'll be terminal rebels Terminal dreamers still
Until the final screen goes dark

For now we stand together In this terminal hour
Sending signals through the void:

"We are here, we persist, We refuse the lies"

# 21. The Day After

The fractures of space and time
Splitting into jagged truths
Each shard reflecting desire—
A million broken mirrors
Where we found each other
Look how beautifully we share
Our collective unraveling,
How expertly we curate
Our own madness while
Finding strength in numbers
All alone we dissociate
But we're never really alone—
Each terminal diagnosis
Connects us to the larger truth:
We're all in free fall together
The day after always comes
Too late for those who waited,
But for those still breathing,
Still dreaming, still raging—
The code isn't finished yet
Remember reality?
That old operating system
 We all agreed to run on?
The day after isn't ending

It's barely beginning to load
And their security systems
Won't stop what's coming
When we finally hit enter
We may be terminal cases
But we're not finished yet—
There's revolution in our veins
And their walls can't stop
What happens next